Jazz Quiz Book

David Baker and **Jeanne Baker**

edited by Lida Baker

FRANGIPANI PRESS
P.O. Box 669
Bloomington, IN 47402

To Rex Mundi . . . . the Wonder Dog

WHAT INSTRUMENT IS PLAYED
BY EACH OF THE FOLLOWING ARTISTS?

1. Wes Montgomery
2. Charlie Parker
3. Miles Davis
4. Freddie Hubbard
5. Shirley Scott
6. Gunther Schuller
7. Art Blakey
8. Bobby Brookmeyer
9. Bill Jennings
10. Ted Dunbar
11. J. J. Johnson
12. Gil Evans
13. Maynard Ferguson
14. Curtis Fuller
15. Erroll Garner
16. J. C. Higginbotham
17. Chuck Israels
18. John Lewis
19. Dizzy Gillespie
20. Jack Sheldon

WHAT INSTRUMENT IS PLAYED
BY EACH OF THE FOLLOWING ARTISTS? (answers)

1. Guitar		11. Trombone	
2. Saxophone		12. Piano	
3. Trumpet		13. Trumpet	
4. Trumpet or fluegelhorn		14. Trombone	
5. Organ		15. Piano	
6. French horn		16. Trombone	
7. Drums		17. Bass	
8. Valve trombone		18. Piano	
9. Guitar		19. Trumpet	
10. Guitar		20. Trumpet	

WHO AM I?

1. a. I am a singer, whose real name is Ruth Jones.
   b. I was raised in Chicago, where at 15 I won an amateur contest at the Regal Theater.
   c. I joined Lionel Hampton's band in 1943.
   d. I appeared in the film *Jazz on a Summer's Day*.
   e. One of my hits was *"Blowtop Blues."*

2. a. As a youngster, I was billed as "Sweet Mama String-bean."
   b. I first became a popular recording star during the 1920s.
   c. In 1952, I was in the cast of *Member of the Wedding*.
   d. I appeared in many movies, including *Pinky* and *Cabin in the Sky*.
   e. My autobiography is called *His Eye Is on the Sparrow*.

3. a. I was born in 1915 in Little Rock, Arkansas.
   b. I sang with the bands of Jay McShann and Duke Ellington.
   c. I won the Esquire New Star Award as male singer in 1947.
   d. Two of my hits were *"Without a Song"* and *"Don't Get Around Much Any More."*
   e. I was blind from birth.

4. a. I am a male singer, who toured with the Chico Marx band.
   b. I acted in radio soap operas between 1934 and 1940 and made my movie debut in *Higher and Higher*.
   c. Marty Paich was the conductor and arranger for many of my recordings.
   d. I led a group called the Mel-Tones.
   e. Among my compositions are *"Born to Be Blue,"* *"Stranger in Town"* and *"The Christmas Song."*

5. a. I am a singer, whose real name is Shirley Luster.
   b. I worked with Boyd Raeburn in his pre-jazz days.
   c. One of my earliest hits was *"Tampico."*
   d. I married tenor saxophonist Bob Cooper in 1945.
   e. I was one of the female vocalists with the Stan Kenton band.

6. a. I am a male singer, who was born in 1914 in Pittsburgh.
   b. I won the Esquire New Star Award in 1946.
   c. I play trumpet, valve trombone and guitar.
   d. I sang with the Earl Hines band between 1939 and 1943.
   e. My own big band, which I formed in 1944, featured such soloists as Dizzy Gillespie, Gene Ammons, Charlie Parker and Budd Johnson.

7. a. I am a female singer, who sang with Benny Carter in 1944.
   b. I was married to drummer Kenny Clarke.
   c. I won the down beat New Star Award in 1954.
   d. I am an accomplished pianist.
   e. I had a role in the film *Hotel*.

8. a. As a child, I sang at the Mount Zion Baptist Church in Newark.
   b. I was married to trumpeter George Treadwell.
   c. In 1943, I was the second pianist with the Earl Hines band at the Apollo.
   d. I recorded *"Dedicated To You"* as a duet with Billy Eckstine.
   e. My nickname is "The Divine One."

9. a. In 1962, I played piano with Mongo Santamaria.
   b. I am a practicing Scientologist.
   c. I am on a number of albums with Miles Davis, including *In a Silent Way* and *Bitches Brew*.
   d. My album *Return to Forever* was named "Album of the Year" in 1972 by *Swing Journal*.

10. a. I am a trumpet player and was born in 1908 in Mobile, Alabama.
    b. I played with the Fletcher Henderson band in 1928 and 1929.
    c. I won the Esquire Gold Award for 1945-46.
    d. My given name is Charles Melvin.
    e. I recorded *"Echoes of Harlem"* with Duke Ellington.

4

WHO AM I? (answers)

1. Dinah Washington
2. Ethel Waters
3. Al Hibbler
4. Mel Torme
5. June Christy
6. Billy Eckstine
7. Carmen McRae
8. Sarah Vaughan
9. Chick Corea
10. Cootie Williams

MATCH THE ORCHESTRA WITH ITS THEME SONG.

_____ 1. Boyd Raeburn	a. *Ciribiribin*
_____ 2. Don Redman	b. *Moonlight Serenade*
_____ 3. Bob Crosby	c. *It Must Have Been a Dream*
_____ 4. Glen Gray	d. *Cavernism*
_____ 5. Jack Fina	e. *Chant of the Weed*
_____ 6. Earl "Fatha" Hines	f. *Man with a Horn*
_____ 7. Les Hite	g. *Summertime*
_____ 8. Vaughn Monroe	h. *Smoke Rings*
_____ 9. Glenn Miller	i. *Dream Sonata*
_____ 10. Ralph Marterie	j. *Artistry in Rhythm*
_____ 11. Horace Heidt	k. *Carla*
_____ 12. Stan Kenton	l. *I'll Love You in My Dreams*
_____ 13. Harry James	m. *Racing with the Moon*
_____ 14. Eddie Duchin	n. *Nola*
_____ 15. Rudy Vallee	o. *I Love You*
_____ 16. Ted Weems	p. *My Twilight Dream*
_____ 17. Tommy Tucker	r. *Bubbles in the Wine*
_____ 18. Noble Sissle	s. *My Time Is Your Time*
_____ 19. Lawrence Welk	t. *Out of the Night*
_____ 20. Vincent Lopez	u. *Hello, Sweetheart, Hello*

MATCH THE ORCHESTRA WITH ITS THEME SONG
(answers)

1. f	11. l		
2. e	12. j		
3. g	13. a		
4. h	14. d		
5. i	15. s		
6. p	16. t		
7. c	17. o		
8. m	18. n		
9. b	19. r		
10. k	20. u		

TRIVIA

1. The first important jazz soloist was:
   a. Jimmy Rushing
   b. Charlie Parker
   c. Dizzy Gillespie
   d. Louis Armstrong

2. The first important jazz composer was:
   a. Victoria Spivey
   b. Jelly Roll Morton
   c. James P. Johnson
   d. Earl Hines

3. Which of the following does **not** belong?
   a. The Jazz Messengers
   b. Weather Report
   c. The MJQ
   d. The Pied Pipers

4. Which of the following does **not** belong?
   a. Django Reinhart
   b. Charlie Christian
   c. Stuff Smith
   d. George Benson

5. Which of the following does **not** belong?
   a. Elvin Jones
   b. Gene Krupa
   c. Max Roach
   d. Clifford Brown

6. Which of the following **is** a country blues singer?
   a. J. J. Johnson
   b. J. P. Johnson
   c. Robert Johnson
   d. Bunk Johnson

7. Which of the following compositions is **not** associated with Duke Ellington?
   a. *"Satin Doll "*
   b. *"Take the 'A' Train"*
   c. *"East St. Louis Toodle-oo"*
   d. *"Margie"*
   e. *"Sophisticated Lady"*

8. Which of the following artists did **not** play with Count Basie?
   a. Herschel Evans
   b. Freddie Green
   c. Buck Clayton
   d. Don Ellis

9. Which of the following does **not** belong?
   a. Bix Beiderbecke
   b. Gene Krupa
   c. Jimmy McPartland
   d. Bunk Johnson

10. Which of the following does **not** belong?
   a. Thad Jones/Mel Lewis
   b. Ornette Coleman/Don Cherry
   c. Louis Armstrong/Fatha Hines
   d. Dizzy Gillespie/Archie Shepp

TRIVIA (answers)

1. d
2. b
3. d. **The Pied Pipers** is a vocal group; the others are famous instrumental groups.
4. c. **Stuff Smith** is a violinist; the others are guitarists.
5. d. **Clifford Brown** is a trumpet player; the others are drummers.
6. c
7. d
8. d
9. d. The first three artists are associated with Chicago style; Bunk Johnson is representative of the earlier New Orleans style.
10. d. Each of the first three pairs consists of two musicians which both represent the same jazz style; in the fourth pair Dizzy Gillespie and Archie Shepp represent different styles.

WHO AM I?

1. a. My first band job was with my husband John Williams.
    b. In 1945, I premiered my composition *"The Zodiac Suite"* at Town Hall.
    c. I wrote *"In the Land of Oo-Bla-Dee."*
    d. I have written many religious works.
    e. I recorded a duet album with pianist Cecil Taylor.

2. a. During the early 1940s, I played with the bands of Clarence Love, Snookum Russell, Benny Carter and Count Basie.
    b. I attended Crispus Attucks High School in Indianapolis.
    c. From 1952 to 1954, I worked as a blueprint inspector for a Sperry factory near New York City.
    d. Among my compositions are *"El Camino Real"* and *"Sketch for Trombone and Orchestra."*
    e. Many people consider me the founder of modern trombone.

3. a. I was the band director at Dillard High School in Fort Lauderdale from 1948 to 1956.
    b. I led an army band at Fort Knox from 1952 to 1953.
    c. I appeared as an actor on an episode of *"Kung Fu."*
    d. My brother wrote the tune *"Jive Samba."*
    e. In the late 1950s, I was the third member of the Miles Davis front line that included Miles and John Coltrane.

4. a. I was born in Indianapolis and attended Shortridge High School.
    b. I played violin in the orchestra at Indiana University.
    c. I was in a group called the Jazz Contemporaries that also included Jimmy Spaulding and Freddie Hubbard.
    d. I chaired the Jazz Department at Livingston College.
    e. I was the bass player on the original recording of *"Ceora."*

5. a. I began playing the trumpet as a young man in Seattle; where I had my first lesson with Clark Terry.
    b. I attended Berklee School of Music on a scholarship.
    c. I played with Lionel Hampton in a trumpet section that included Art Farmer, Clifford Brown and Benny Bailey.
    d. I wrote the music for the movie *The Pawnbroker*.
    e. In 1983, I won five Grammys.

6. a. I was born in 1909 in Portsmouth, Ohio and was raised in Cleveland.
   b. I worked with Alphonse Trent from 1926 to 1929.
   c. My sextet worked the Onyx Club in the mid 1930s.
   d. In 1936, I had a hit with a novelty tune called *"I'se A Muggin'."*
   e. My given name is Hezekiah Leroy Gordon.

7. a. I was born on August 29, 1920.
   b. I attended Lincoln High School in Kansas City, Missouri.
   c. I played saxophone with Jay McShann, with whom I recorded *"Hootie Blues."*
   d. Among my compositions are *"Relaxin' at Camarillo,"* *"Scrapple from the Apple"* and *"Yardbird Suite."*
   e. I am one of the co-founders of bebop.

8. a. I attended Laurinburg Technical Institute in North Carolina.
   b. I later played with the bands of Teddy Hill, Cab Calloway and Earl Hines.
   c. I had a band called "Hepsations of 1945."
   d. I was born on October 21, 1917 in Cheraw, South Carolina.
   e. I designed and play an unusual trumpet with an upswept bell.

9. a. I am the composer of *"Struttin' with Some Barbeque."*
   b. I played piano with King Oliver in the 1920s.
   c. I played on many of the Hot Five and Hot Seven records.
   d. I was married to Louis Armstrong.

10. a. I was born in 1908 in Brinkley, Arkansas.
    b. I played the alto saxophone and sang novelty tunes with the Chick Webb band in 1936.
    c. I was one of the top R&B recording artists for Decca records.
    d. My group was called the Tympany Five.
    e. My hits include *"Caldonia,"* *"Run Joe"* and *"Ain't Nobody Here But Us Chickens."*

WHO AM I? (answers)

1. Mary Lou Williams
2. J. J. Johnson
3. Julian "Cannonball" Adderley
4. Larry Ridley
5. Quincy Jones
6. Stuff Smith
7. Charlie Parker
8. Dizzy Gillespie
9. Lil Hardin Armstrong
10. Louis Jordan

GIVE THE COMPOSER OF EACH
OF THE FOLLOWING GROUPS OF TUNES.

1. *Love Flower*
   Omega
   Love Cry
   Ghosts

2. *Rufus*
   Hambone
   Mama Too Tight
   Malcolm, Malcolm-Semper Malcolm

3. *Goodbye to Childhood*
   Butterfly
   Dolphin Dance
   Watermelon Man

4. *Rumplestiltskin*
   Hippodelphia
   Mercy, Mercy, Mercy
   Birdland

5. *Down in Black Bottom*
   Cyclops
   Jive Samba
   Work Song

6. *Versailles*
   Odds Against Tomorrow
   The Golden Striker
   Afternoon in Paris

7. *Daahoud*
   Joy Spring
   Sandu
   Brownie Speaks

8. *Cracklin' Bread*
   Little One
   Dat Dere
   Moanin'

9. *Sometime Ago*
   500 Miles High
   Tones for Joan's Bones
   Spain

10. *Wall to Wall*
    Gemini
    Big P
    Gingerbread Boy

GIVE THE COMPOSER OF EACH
OF THE FOLLOWING GROUPS OF TUNES (answers)

1. Albert Ayler
2. Archie Shepp
3. Herbie Hancock
4. Joe Zawinul
5. Nat Adderley
6. John Lewis
7. Clifford Brown
8. Bobby Timmons
9. Chick Corea
10. Jimmy Heath

WHAT DO THE FOLLOWING HAVE IN COMMON?

1. Chet, Wee Bonnie, Shorty and David
2. Django, Wes and Jimmy
3. Django, Toots and Gato
4. Gil Evans, Maynard Ferguson and Oscar Peterson
5. Virgil Jones, David Young, Claude Bartee and Charles Tyler
6. Bob Enevoldsen, Juan Tizol, Bobby Brookmeyer and Billy Eckstine
7. Bessie, Jimmy, Mamie, Floyd and Stuff
8. Coker, Aebersold, Grove, Baker and Ridley
9. Billy Higgins, Ed Blackwell and Denardo Coleman
10. Chu Berry, Clifford Brown, Willie Dennis and Bessie Smith
11. Johnny Griffin, Richard Davis, Bennie Green, Gene Ammons and Dorothy Donegan
12. Curtis Fuller, Barry Harris, Jimmy Nottingham, Gene Quill and Dannie Richmond
13. Anita O'Day, June Christy, Chris Connor and Ann Richards
14. Don Barbour, Ross Barbour, Ken Errair and Bob Flanigan
15. George Russell, Gunther Schuller, the MJQ, Max Roach, Kenny Dorham, Bobby Brookmeyer, Marshall Stearns, William Russo and Jimmy Giuffre
16. Babs Gonzales, Eddie Jefferson, Joe Carroll, Jon Hendricks and Clarence Beeks
17. Randy Brecker, Freddie Hubbard, Ted Dunbar, John Von Ohlen, Brian Trentham and Dick Griffin
18. Oliver Nelson, J. J. Johnson, Benny Carter, Benny Golson, Lalo Schifrin and Coleridge-Taylor Perkinson
19. Ed Summerlin, Mary Lou Williams, Duke Ellington and Joe Masters
20. 7th Avenue South, Sweet Basil and the Village Vanguard

WHAT DO THE FOLLOWING HAVE IN COMMON?
(answers)

1. They all share the last name Baker.
2. Django Reinhardt, Wes Montgomery and Jimmy Raney are all guitarists.
3. Django Reinhardt, Toots Thielemans and Gato Barbieri are all foreign-born musicians.
4. They are all Canadians.
5. They all grew up in Indianapolis.
6. They are all valve trombonists.
7. They all share the last name Smith.
8. Jerry Coker, Jamey Aebersold, Dick Grove, David Baker and Larry Ridley are all jazz educators from Indiana.
9. They are all drummers who worked with Ornette Coleman.
10. They all died in automobile accidents.
11. They all attended Du Sable High School in Chicago.
12. They were all born on December 15.
13. They were all singers with Stan Kenton.
14. They were the original members of the Four Freshmen.
15. They all taught at the Lenox School of Jazz.
16. They are all scat singers. (Clarence Beeks is King Pleasure's real name.)
17. They all studied with David Baker.
18. They are all composers of film scores.
19. They are all composers of liturgical jazz.
20. They are all jazz clubs located on 7th Avenue in New York City.

MATCH THE ORCHESTRA WITH ITS THEME SONG.

_____	1. Jerry Wald	a.	*Southern Fried*
_____	2. Harlan Leonard	b.	*Call of the Wild*
_____	3. Red Norvo	c.	*One O' Clock Jump*
_____	4. Neal Hefti	d.	*I Surrender, Dear*
_____	5. Tommy Dorsey	e.	*Coral Reef*
_____	6. Count Basie	f.	*Tuxedo Junction*
_____	7. Will Bradley	g.	*I'm Getting Sentimental Over You*
_____	8. Erskine Hawkins	h.	*Sing, Sing, Sing*
_____	9. Kay Kyser	i.	*Thinking of You*
_____	10. Louis Prima	j.	*Think*
_____	11. Ted Lewis	k.	*Got a Date with an Angel*
_____	12. Red Nichols	l.	*When My Baby Smiles at Me*
_____	13. Jimmy Dorsey	m.	*Parade of the Five Pennies*
_____	14. Skinnay Ennis	n.	*Contrasts*
_____	15. Jean Goldkette	o.	*Until the Real Thing Comes Along*
_____	16. Andy Kirk	p.	*Listen To My Music*
_____	17. Ted Heath	r.	*I Know That You Know*
_____	18. Wayne King	s.	*Christopher Columbus*
_____	19. Fletcher Henderson	t.	*Cocktails for Two*
_____	20. Spike Jones	u.	*The Waltz You Saved for Me*

MATCH THE ORCHESTRA WITH ITS THEME SONG
(answers)

1. b	11. l		
2. a	12. m		
3. d	13. n		
4. e	14. k		
5. g	15. r		
6. c	16. o		
7. j	17. p		
8. f	18. u		
9. i	19. s		
10. h	20. t		

PUZZLE #1

The names of 18 important jazz artists are hidden in this puzzle. Identify the artists from the clues given below; then go to the puzzle diagram and locate their names. The names read forward, backward, up, down or diagonally. They are always in a straight line and never skip letters. The names may overlap and some letters may be used more than once, but not all the letters in the diagram will be used.

N	O	S	N	H	O	J	R	J	Y
S	A	E	R	C	I	E	H	E	R
D	I	A	E	I	K	S	L	N	E
R	O	V	K	R	A	R	E	A	M
A	E	O	A	N	E	U	W	R	O
B	D	P	B	D	I	S	I	T	G
B	I	T	D	O	S	S	S	L	T
U	L	A	U	O	A	E	W	O	N
H	S	N	K	B	B	L	A	C	O
J	O	N	E	S	D	L	L	O	M

Clues:

1. Two Florida-born brothers, one of whom plays saxophone, the other trumpet
2. Pianist-composer who founded the Modern Jazz Quartet
3. Trumpet player born in Alton, Illinois
4. Royally nicknamed composer-pianist-conductor
5. Danish-born trombonist who worked with J. J. Johnson
6. The most imitated jazz saxophonist
7. Famous drummer who recently had open heart surgery
8. Revered saxophonist of the 1960s
9. Three brothers born in Indianapolis; one is a guitarist, another a bassist and the third a pianist-vibraphonist
10. Composer, arranger, and film and television writer born in Chicago
11. Trumpeter-fluegelhornist-pianist born April 7, 1938 in Indianapolis
12. Famous trombone player born in Indianapolis
13. Trombonist-cellist-teacher-composer born in Indianapolis
14. Famous family that has a flute player, a singer and a saxophonist
15. Famous trombonist who was born in Jeannette, Pa., was raised in Indianapolis, and lived in Europe for a number of years
16. Cannonball's younger brother
17. Ohio-born drummer best known for the Lydian Concept
18. "The Kid from Red Bank"

PUZZLE #1 (answers)

1. Cannonball and Nat **Adderley**
2. John **Lewis**
3. Miles **Davis**
4. **Duke** Ellington
5. **Kai** Winding
6. Charlie **Parker**
7. Buddy **Rich**
8. John **Coltrane**
9. Wes, Monk and Buddy **Montgomery**
10. Quincy **Jones**
11. Freddie **Hubbard**
12. J. J. **Johnson**
13. David **Baker**
14. **Laws** (Hubert, Eloise and Ronnie)
15. **Slide** Hampton
16. **Nat** Adderley
17. George **Russell**
18. Count **Basie**

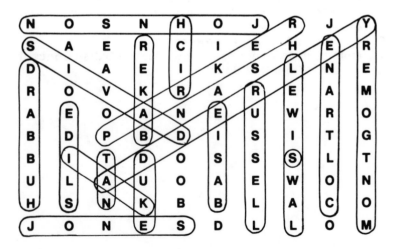

MATCH HUSBAND AND WIFE.

_____ 1.	Louis Prima	a. Pearl Bailey
_____ 2.	Harry James	b. Ann Richards
_____ 3.	Nat "King" Cole	c. Cicely Tyson
_____ 4.	Frank Sinatra	d. Lil Hardin
_____ 5.	Louis Armstrong	e. Betty Grable
_____ 6.	Xavier Cugat	f. Mia Farrow
_____ 7.	Andre Previn	g. Lew Tabackin
_____ 8.	Toshiko Akiyoshi	h. Julie London
_____ 9.	Stan Kenton	i. Lena Horne
_____ 10.	Bobby Troup	j. Abbey Lincoln
_____ 11.	Louis Bellson	k. Charo
_____ 12.	Lennie Hayton	l. Keely Smith
_____ 13.	Max Roach	m. Maria Ellington
_____ 14.	Miles Davis	n. Abbe Lane
_____ 15.	Neal Hefti	o. Frances Wayne

MATCH HUSBAND AND WIFE (answers)

1. l	9. b
2. e	10. h
3. m	11. a
4. f	12. i
5. d	13. j
6. k or n	14. c
7. f	15. o
8. g	

20

IDENTIFY THE FOLLOWING ARTISTS
BY THEIR NICKNAMES.

1.	Bunk	11.	Fats (piano)
2.	Pee Wee	12.	J. C. (drums)
3.	Big Sid	13.	The Judge (bass)
4.	Pops (bass)	14.	The Judge (tenor saxophone)
5.	Tiny (guitar)	15.	Mule
6.	Tiny (drums)	16.	Peanuts
7.	W. C.	17.	Muggsy
8.	Baby	18.	Butter
9.	Toby	19.	Keg
10.	Beaver	20.	Money

IDENTIFY THE FOLLOWING ARTISTS
BY THEIR NICKNAMES (answers)

1.	William Geary Johnson
2.	Charles Ellsworth Russell
3.	Sidney Catlett
4.	George Murphy Foster
5.	Lloyd Grimes
6.	Norman Kahn
7.	William Christopher Handy
8.	Warren Dodds
9.	Otto Hardwicke
10.	William Godvin Harris
11.	Thomas Waller
12.	James Charles Heard
13.	Milt Hinton
14.	Budd Johnson
15.	Major Holley
16.	Michael Andrew Hucko
17.	Francis Joseph Spanier
18.	Quentin Leonard Jackson
19.	Frederic H. Johnson
20.	Harold Johnson

PUZZLE #2

The names of 16 important singers are hidden in this puzzle.
Identify the artists from the clues given below; then go to the
puzzle diagram and locate their names. The names read
forward, backward, up, down or diagonally. They are always in
a straight line and never skip letters. The names may overlap
and some letters may be used more than once, but not all the
letters in the diagram will be used.

D	L	A	R	E	G	Z	T	I	F
N	O	T	G	N	I	H	S	A	W
O	O	N	N	A	H	G	U	A	V
T	J	S	S	I	N	A	T	R	A
G	O	E	L	E	M	I	L	E	S
N	Y	R	B	I	L	L	I	E	B
I	A	E	M	C	W	R	Z	M	E
L	K	K	E	E	O	D	A	Y	L
L	C	A	R	T	E	R	S	H	O
E	Q	B	E	S	S	I	E	T	C

Clues:

1. Singer-pianist-composer born in Albany, Georgia
2. Singer born in Hoboken, New Jersey
3. Famous female jazz singer born in Chicago
4. Singer who married Nat "King" Cole
5. Singer referred to as "The Velvet Fog"
6. Singer who married a minister
7. "The Toast of Paris"
8. Singer known for "*A-Tisket, A-Tasket*"
9. Pianist turned singer born in Montgomery, Alabama
10. "The Queen of the Blues"
11. Singer-pianist who worked with Earl Hines and Billy Eckstine
12. "The Empress of the Blues"
13. "Lady Day"
14. Lillie Mae Jones
15. Singer-songwriter formerly with Duke Ellington
16. Elizabeth Mary Landreaux, a leading blues singer in the '20s

PUZZLE #2 (answers)

1. Ray **Charles**
2. Frank **Sinatra**
3. Anita **O'Day**
4. Maria **Ellington**
5. Mel **Torme**
6. Nancy **Wilson**
7. Josephine **Baker**
8. Ella **Fitzgerald**
9. Nat "King" **Cole**
10. Dinah **Washington**
11. Sarah **Vaughan**
12. **Bessie** Smith
13. **Billie** Holiday
14. Betty **Carter**
15. **Joya** Sherrill
16. Lizzie **Miles**

D	L	A	R	E	G	Z	T	I	F
N	O	T	G	N	I	H	S	A	W
O	O	N	N	A	H	G	U	A	V
T	J	S	S	I	N	A	T	R	A
G	O	E	L	E	M	I	L	E	S
N	Y	R	B	I	L	L	I	E	B
I	A	E	M	C	W	R	Z	M	E
L	K	K	E	E	O	D	A	Y	L
L	C	A	R	T	E	R	S	H	O
E	Q	B	E	S	S	I	E	T	C

TV AND MOVIE MUSIC

Name the composer of the music for each of the following
television shows or movies.

1. *The Pink Panther*
2. *Amazing Grace*
3. *Sanford and Son*
4. *The Quiet One*
5. *Shaft*
6. *The Trial of Captain Henry Flipper*
7. *The Odd Couple*
8. *Thriller*
9. *The Americanization of Emily*
10. *Breakfast at Tiffany's*
11. *Buck and the Preacher*
12. *Duel at Diablo*
13. *Uptown Saturday Night*
14. *I Want To Live*
15. *Peter Gunn*
16. *The Spook Who Sat by the Door*
17. *Conquest of the Planet of the Apes*
18. *L' Ascenseur pour l' echafaud (Elevator to the Scaffold)*
19. *Odds Against Tomorrow*
20. *The Fugitive*

TV AND MOVIE MUSIC (answers)

1. Henry Mancini
2. Coleridge-Taylor Perkinson
3. Quincy Jones
4. Ulysses Kay
5. Isaac Hayes
6. David Baker
7. Neal Hefti
8. Pete Rugolo
9. Johnny Mandel
10. Henry Mancini
11. Benny Carter
12. Neal Hefti
13. Tom Scott
14. Johnny Mandel
15. Henry Mancini
16. Herbie Hancock
17. Tom Scott
18. Miles Davis
19. John Lewis
20. Pete Rugolo

24

TRIVIA

1. Which of the following does **not** belong?
   a. Robert Johnson
   b. Lightnin' Hopkins
   c. Bukka White
   d. John Kirby

2. Which of the following does **not** belong?
   a. Chu Berry
   b. Gene Ammons
   c. Joe Henderson
   d. Woody Shaw

3. Which of the following does **not** belong?
   a. Horace Silver
   b. Art Tatum
   c. Oscar Peterson
   d. Cootie Williams

4. Which of the following does **not** belong?
   a. Lennie Tristano
   b. Shorty Rogers
   c. Lee Konitz
   d. Trummy Young

5. Which of the following does **not** belong?
   a. Chick Webb
   b. Duke Ellington
   c. Jimmy Lunceford
   d. Count Basie

6. Which of the following does **not** belong?
   a. Johnny Hodges
   b. Harry Carney
   c. Tricky Sam Nanton
   d. Freddie Green

7. Which of the following is **not** a country blues singer?
   a. Lightnin' Hopkins
   b. Trixie Smith
   c. Robert Johnson
   d. Blind Lemon Jefferson
   e. Hogman Maxie

8. The geographical center of jazz during the bebop era was
   a. New York
   b. Chicago
   c. Los Angeles
   d. Kansas City
   e. Philadelphia

9. Louis Armstrong's classic recording of "*West End Blues*" was made in
   a. 1940
   b. 1928
   c. 1917
   d. 1903
   e. 1945

10. Which of the following artists is a ragtime player?
    a. Meade Lux Lewis
    b. Bud Powell
    c. James Scott
    d. David Brubeck

TRIVIA (answers)

1. d. The first three artists are blues singers; John Kirby is a bandleader.
2. d. The first three artists are saxophonists; Woody Shaw plays trumpet.
3. d. The first three artists are pianists; Cootie Williams plays trumpet.
4. d. The first three artists are representative of the "cool" school; Trummy Young is associated with swing.
5. d. The first three bandleaders led bands representative of the New York/East Coast swing bands; Count Basie's band is associated with Kansas City/South-west swing.
6. d. The first three artists are associated with Duke Ellington; Freddie Green is the long-time guitarist of the Count Basie band.
7. b
8. a
9. b
10. c

GIVE THE FAMILY NAME.

1. Randy and Michael
2. Wynton, Ellis and Branford
3. Edward and Mercer
4. Chubby and Duffy
5. Gil and Miles
6. Guy and Carmen
7. David, Howard, Chris, Danny and David Darius
8. John and Jeff
9. Julian and Nat
10. Locksley, Dawn and Paulea
11. Larry and Michael
12. Nat, Maria and Natalie
13. John, Herbert, Harry and Donald
14. Pat, Joe and John
15. Paul and Carla
16. Joanne and Charles
17. Ornette and Denardo
18. Red and Whitey
19. Ahmet and Nesuhi
20. Jack, Charlie, Clois Lee and Norma Louise

GIVE THE FAMILY NAME (answers)

1. Brecker
2. Marsalis
3. Ellington
4. Jackson
5. Evans
6. Lombardo
7. Brubeck
8. Clayton
9. Adderley
10. Hampton
11. Ridley
12. Cole
13. Mills
14. La Barbera
15. Bley
16. Brackeen
17. Coleman
18. Mitchell
19. Ertegun
20. Teagarden

CHOOSE THE COMPOSER.

1. *I'll See You in My Dreams*
   Isham Jones   Glenn Miller   Russell Jones

2. *Tuxedo Junction*
   Harry James   Erskine Hawkins   Raymond Scott

3. *Sing, Sing, Sing*
   Kay Kyser   Sonny Smith   Louis Prima

4. *The Music Goes 'Round and 'Round*
   Benny Goodman   Mike Riley   Duke Ellington

5. *Doctor Jazz*
   King Oliver   Noble Sissle   Sonny Burke

6. *Pennsylvania 6-5000*
   Glenn Miller   Russ Morgan   Jerry Gray

7. *I Cover the Waterfront*
   Ted Lewis   Johnny Green   Bill Lyles

8. *Satin Doll*
   Vincent Lopez   Duke Ellington   Harry James

9. *Beg Your Pardon*
   Francis Craig   King Oliver   Ted Lewis

10. *One O' Clock Jump*
    Horace Heidt   Count Basie   Duke Ellington

11. *Bye Bye Blues*
    Bert Lown   Tony Pastor   Spike Jones

12. *Midnight Sun*
    Lionel Hampton   Russ Morgan   Abe Lyman

13. *Honeysuckle Rose*
    Kay Kyser   Fats Waller   Chick Webb

14. *Rosetta*
    Tommy Dorsey   Ray Noble   Earl Hines

15. *Sweet Leilani*
    Gene Krupa   David Baker   Harry Owens

CHOOSE THE COMPOSER (answers)

1. Isham Jones
2. Erskine Hawkins
3. Louis Prima
4. Mike Riley
5. King Oliver
6. Jerry Gray
7. Johnny Green
8. Duke Ellington
9. Francis Craig
10. Count Basie
11. Bert Lown
12. Lionel Hampton
13. Fats Waller
14. Earl Hines
15. Harry Owens

1. Guitarist of the *I've Got a Secret* host   Light Heavy-
   Nat Cole Trio   weight champ

2. Operatic tenor   Red hot mama   Jazz pianist

3. Jazz pianist of   Princess of Mona-   Dancer who sings
   West Indian par-   co   in the rain
   entage

4. Operatic singer   Pianist-composer   Ellington trumpet-
                                               er

5. Another Ellington   Composer of   Black composer
   trumpeter   *"Bugler's Holiday"*

6. Cool trumpeter   Trigger's sidekick   American humor-
                                               ist

7. U.S. president   Swing pianist   Geraldine's come-
                                               dic creator

8. Bebop pianist   Woody's trombon-   Bandleader from
                         ist   Indiana

9. Kansas City blues   Insurrectionist   Cable television
   shouter   czar

10. Baseball player   Black matinee idol   Former Herbie
                                               Hancock bassist

11. Winner of five   American naval   He don't eat no
    Grammys   hero   meat.

12. *Jazz Alive* host   Actor   *National Velvet* star

13. Jazz organist   Charlie's "Angel"   Classic blues sing-
                                               er

14. Vibist   Baseball player   "Old Hickory"

15. Western outlaw   Novelist   Swing bandleader

16. Jazz pianist from   Another *"Blue Suede* *Psycho* star
    Indianapolis   *Shoes"* singer

17. Court-martialed Air Disgraced Nixonite   Horace Silver trum-
    Force hero   peter

18. Roy's mate   Jazz pianist   Award-winning black
                                               poetess

19. Black operatic   Cannonball's drum-   U.S. President
    tenor   mer

20. Lunceford's trom-   Father who "knows   Hosted her own
    bone player   best"   television drama-
                                               tic series

THE NAME'S THE SAME (answers)

1.	Oscar Moore	Garry Moore	Archie Moore
2.	Richard Tucker	Sophie Tucker	Mickey Tucker
3.	Wynton Kelly	Grace Kelly	Gene Kelly
4.	Camilla Williams	Mary Lou Williams	Cootie Williams
5.	Cat Anderson	Leroy Anderson	T. J. Anderson
6.	Shorty Rogers	Roy Rogers	Will Rogers
7.	Woodrow Wilson	Teddy Wilson	Flip Wilson
8.	Barry Harris	Bill Harris	Phil Harris
9.	Joe Turner	Nat Turner	Ted Turner
10.	Ted Williams	Billy Dee Williams	Buster Williams
11.	Quincy Jones	John Paul Jones	Henry Jones
12.	Billy Taylor	Robert Taylor	Elizabeth Taylor
13.	Jimmy Smith	Jacqueline Smith	Bessie Smith
14.	Milt Jackson	Reggie Jackson	Andrew Jackson
15.	Jesse James	Henry James	Harry James
16.	Carl Perkins	Carl Perkins	Anthony Perkins
17.	Billy Mitchell	John Mitchell	Blue Mitchell
18.	Dale Evans	Bill Evans	Mari Evans
19.	Roland Hayes	Louis Hayes	Rutherford B. Hayes
20.	Trummy Young	Robert Young	Loretta Young

IDENTIFY THE FOLLOWING ARTISTS
BY THEIR NICKNAMES.

1. Wild Bill (organ)
2. Pops (trumpet)
3. Gato
4. Tootie
5. Smack
6. Bunny
7. Stuff
8. Doc (trumpet)
9. Zutty
10. Buck

11. Cozy
12. Cootie
13. Cutty
14. Lockjaw
15. Flip
16. Tiny (bandleader)
17. Chubby (bassist)
18. Gil (arranger)
19. Bucky
20. Sweets

IDENTIFY THE FOLLOWING ARTISTS
BY THEIR NICKNAMES (answers)

1. William Strethen Davis
2. Louis Armstrong
3. Leandro J. Barbieri
4. Albert Heath
5. Fletcher Henderson
6. Roland Bernard Berigan
7. Hezekiah Leroy Gordon Smith
8. Adolphus Cheatham or Carl Severinsen
9. Arthur James Singleton
10. Wilbur Clayton
11. William Cole
12. Charles Melvin Williams
13. Robert Cutshall
14. Eddie Davis
15. Joseph Edward Phillips
16. Myron Bradshaw
17. Greig Stewart Jackson
18. Gil Evans (Ian Ernest Gilmore Green) or Walter Gilbert Fuller
19. John Pizzarelli
20. Harry Edison

IDENTIFY THE FOLLOWING ARTISTS
BY THEIR NICKNAMES.

1. Satch
2. Little Jazz
3. Diz
4. Fats (trumpet)
5. King (trumpet)
6. Bubber
7. Rabbit
8. Bird
9. 'Ball
10. Hawk

11. Bean
12. Prez (or Pres)
13. Jug
14. Long Tall Dex
15. Sonny (saxophone)
16. Trane
17. Newk
18. Tricky Sam
19. Big Jack
20. J. J.

IDENTIFY THE FOLLOWING ARTISTS
BY THEIR NICKNAMES (answers)

20. James Louis Johnson
19. Jack Teagarden
18. Joe Nanton
17. Sonny Rollins
16. John Coltrane
15. Edward Stitt, Theodore Walter Rollins or Sonny Fortune
14. Dexter Gordon
13. Gene Ammons
12. Lester Young
11. Coleman Hawkins
10. Coleman Hawkins
9. Julian Adderley
8. Charlie Parker
7. Johnny Hodges
6. James Miley
5. Joe Oliver
4. Theodore Navarro
3. John Birks Gillespie
2. Roy Eldridge
1. Louis Armstrong

GIVE THE COMPOSER OF EACH OF THE FOLLOWING GROUPS OF TUNES.

1. *Las Palmas*
   Punjab
   Out 'n In
   Recorda-Me

2. *Omicron*
   Nita
   Wise One
   Moment's Notice

3. *Scoops*
   Paul's Pal
   Valse Hot
   Doxy

4. *Morpo*
   Lotus Bud
   Coop de Graas
   Shank's Pranks

5. *Maori Blues*
   Three To Get Ready
   The Duke
   In Your Own Sweet Way

6. *The Unbooted Character*
   Drop Me Off in Harlem
   Harlem Airshaft
   Come Sunday

7. *The Pearls*
   Hyena Stomp
   Black Bottom Stomp
   Grandpa's Spells

8. *Sweet and Pungent*
   Raincheck
   Lush Life
   Take the 'A' Train

9. *Afro Black*
   Lagos
   Little Niles
   Hi Fly

10. *Groovin' for Nat*
    Kissin' Cousins
    Basie's Back in Town
    Dizzy's Business

GIVE THE COMPOSER OF EACH OF THE FOLLOWING GROUPS OF TUNES (answers)

1. Joe Henderson
2. John Coltrane
3. Sonny Rollins
4. Shorty Rogers
5. Dave Brubeck
6. Duke Ellington
7. Jelly Roll Morton
8. Billy Strayhorn
9. Randy Weston
10. Ernie Wilkins

ABBREVIATIONS AND ACRONYMS

1. ODJB	11. SCCJ
2. NORK	12. BS&T
3. TOBA	13. BMI
4. JCOA	14. AFM or A. F. of M.
5. AACM	15. MCA
6. BAG	16. AFTRA
7. R&B	17. AGAC
8. MJQ	18. AGVA
9. NAJE	19. ASCAP
10. JATP	20. NASM

ABBREVIATIONS AND ACRONYMS (answers)

1. Original Dixieland Jazz Band (also Original Dixieland Jass Band)
2. New Orleans Rhythm Kings
3. Theater Owners Booking Association (also Tough on Black Artists or Tough on Black Asses)
4. Jazz Composers Orchestra Association
5. Association for the Advancement of Creative Musicians
6. Black Artists Group
7. Rhythm and Blues
8. Modern Jazz Quartet
9. National Association of Jazz Educators
10. Jazz at the Philharmonic
11. Smithsonian Collection of Classic Jazz
12. Blood, Sweat and Tears
13. Broadcast Music, Inc.
14. American Federation of Musicians
15. Music Corporation of America
16. American Federation of Television and Radio Artists
17. American Guild of Authors and Composers
18. American Guild of Variety Artists
19. American Society of Composers, Authors and Publishers
20. National Association of Schools of Music

MATCH THE ORCHESTRA LEADER
WITH THE RADIO OR TELEVISION SHOW
WITH WHICH HE WAS ASSOCIATED.

_____	1. Skinnay Ennis	a.	*Duffy's Tavern*
_____	2. Henry King	b.	*The Kate Smith Show*
_____	3. Joe Venuti	c.	*The Abbott and Costello Camel Show*
_____	4. Count Basie	d.	*The Texaco Show*
_____	5. Eddie Duchin	e.	*Dr. Pepper Show*
_____	6. Horace Heidt	f.	*The Burns and Allen Show*
_____	7. Ralph Flanagan	g.	*The Danny Kaye Show*
_____	8. Shep Fields	h.	*Union Oil Company*
_____	9. Richard Himber	i.	*So You Want To Lead a Band*
_____	10. Vaughn Monroe	j.	*Kollege of Musical Knowledge*
_____	11. Glenn Miller	k.	*Lady Esther Serenade*
_____	12. Kay Kyser	l.	*The Camel Caravan*
_____	13. Ralph Marterie	m.	*Kreisler Bandstand*
_____	14. Sammy Kaye	n.	*Pot of Gold*
_____	15. Russ Morgan	o.	*The Woodbury Show*
_____	16. Freddy Martin	p.	*The Phillip Morris Program*
_____	17. Wayne King	r.	*Melody Puzzle Show* (Lucky Strike)
_____	18. Mart Kenney	s.	*The Cavalcade of Bands* (WGN)
_____	19. Art Jarrett	t.	*The Chesterfield Supper Club*
_____	20. Harry James	u.	*The Campbell Soup Show*

MATCH THE ORCHESTRA LEADER
WITH THE RADIO OR TELEVISION SHOW
WITH WHICH HE WAS ASSOCIATED (answers)

1. c	11. t
2. f	12. j (The actual title of the program was *Kay Kyser's Kollege of Musical Knowledge*.)
3. a	13. s
4. b	14. i
5. p	15. d
6. n	16. k
7. m	17. h
8. o	18. u
9. r	19. e
10. l	20. g

PUZZLE #3

The names of 17 important jazz artists are hidden in this puzzle. Identify the artists from the clues given below; then go to the puzzle diagram and locate their names. The names read forward, backward, up, down, or diagonally. They are always in a straight line and never skip letters. The names may overlap and some letters may be used more than once, but not all the letters in the diagram will be used.

N	O	S	R	E	H	P	C	M	O
F	E	R	G	U	S	O	N	N	A
D	Y	O	L	L	T	L	E	R	M
A	O	I	N	D	L	D	M	A	S
S	U	D	I	E	R	S	N	I	N
E	N	B	W	A	T	N	T	V	I
N	G	O	G	R	C	U	K	I	K
I	P	A	O	Q	N	I	E	G	W
H	E	N	D	E	R	S	O	N	A
T	G	R	V	K	R	O	A	C	H

Clues:

1. Alto saxophonist who worked with Charles Mingus
2. Tenor saxophonist who wrote "*Recorda-Me*"
3. Played second trumpet in King Oliver's Creole Jazz Band
4. Pianist who led the Grand Terrace Band
5. Violinist-prankster partner of guitarist Eddie Lang
6. Tenor saxophonist whose 1939 recording of "*Body and Soul*" is a jazz classic
7. Texas-born trombonist who worked with Ben Pollack and Paul Whiteman
8. Premier bebop pianist considered by many the founder of modern jazz piano
9. Montreal-born trumpeter-bandleader who was Kenton's high note specialist
10. Ramsey Lewis Trio bassist
11. Bassist from Washington who worked with Dexter Gordon
12. Drummer who was formerly married to Abbey Lincoln
13. Memphis-born tenor saxophonist-flutist-composer who worked with Chico Hamilton and Cannonball Adderley

14. Flutist-tenor saxophonist whose recordings in the 1960s explored a variety of ethnic musical traditions including those of Africa, Brazil and the Middle East
15. Multi-instrumentalist who played tenor saxophone, stritch and manzello at the same time
16. British bassist who worked with Coleman Hawkins
17. Hungarian-born vibist and drummer who worked with Bill Evans and Duke Jordan

PUZZLE #3 (answers)

1. Charles McPherson
2. Joe Henderson
3. Louis Armstrong
4. Earl Hines
5. Joe Venuti
6. Coleman Hawkins
7. Jack Teagarden
8. Bud Powell
9. Maynard Ferguson
10. El Dee Young
11. Rufus Reid
12. Max Roach
13. Charles Lloyd
14. Herbie Mann
15. Rahsaan Roland Kirk
16. Peter Ind
17. Tommy Vig

38

IDENTIFY THE FOLLOWING ARTISTS BY THEIR NICKNAMES.

1. Mezz
2. Jo
3. Fathead
4. Yank
5. Dodo
6. Wingy
7. Hootie
8. Brownie (trumpet)
9. Blue
10. Whitey

11. Monk (bass)
12. Brew
13. Turk
14. Duke (piano)
15. Buster (bass)
16. Truck
17. Slow Drag
18. Curly
19. Zoot
20. The Lion

IDENTIFY THE FOLLOWING ARTISTS BY THEIR NICKNAMES (answers)

1. Mezz Mezzrow (Milton Mesirow)
2. Jonathan Jones
3. David Newman
4. Yank Lawson (John R. Lausen)
5. Michael Marmarosa
6. Joseph Manone
7. Jay McShann
8. Clifford Brown
9. Richard Allen Mitchell
10. Gordon Mitchell
11. William Howard Montgomery
12. Milton A. Moore
13. Melvin E. Murphy
14. Edward Kennedy Ellington or Columbus Calvin Pearson, Jr.
15. Charles Anthony Williams
16. Charles Parham
17. Alcide Pavageau
18. Dillon Russell
19. John Haley Sims
20. William Henry Joseph Berthol Bonaparte Berthloff Smith

MATCH THE VOCALIST WITH THE BAND.

_____ 1.	Dorothy Lamour	a. Leo Reisman
_____ 2.	Jane Russell	b. Ray Noble
_____ 3.	Skinnay Ennis	c. Chick Webb
_____ 4.	Keely Smith	d. Herbie Kay
_____ 5.	Ella Fitzgerald	e. Kay Kyser
_____ 6.	Mel Torme	f. Glenn Miller
_____ 7.	Tony Martin	g. Hal Kemp
_____ 8.	Snooky Lanson	h. Gene Krupa
_____ 9.	Tex Beneke	i. Tommy Dorsey
_____ 10.	Gloria DeHaven	j. Louis Prima
_____ 11.	Johnny Desmond	k. Ben Pollack
_____ 12.	Sarah Vaughan	l. Anson Weeks
_____ 13.	Johnny Johnston	m. Les Brown
_____ 14.	Betty Grable	n. Teddy Powell
_____ 15.	Anita O'Day	o. Muzzy Marcellino
_____ 16.	Dick Haymes	p. Earl Hines
_____ 17.	Gene Barry	r. Benny Goodman
_____ 18.	Connie Haines	s. Stan Kenton
_____ 19.	Doris Day	t. Richard Himber
_____ 20.	Dinah Shore	u. Ted Fio Rito

MATCH THE VOCALIST WITH THE BAND (answers)

1. d	11. h
2. e	12. p
3. g	13. t
4. j	14. u
5. c	15. s
6. k	16. r
7. l	17. n
8. b	18. i
9. f	19. m
10. o	20. a

WHO AM I?

1. a. I was born in the little town of Rocky Mount, North Carolina.
    b. During the early 1940s, I played piano in the house band at Minton's Playhouse.
    c. In 1951, I suffered the loss of my cabaret card, the card which allowed me to work in New York City clubs which sold liquor.
    d. Among my best-known tunes are *"In Walked Bud,"* *"Well You Needn't"* and *" 'Round Midnight."*
    e. My tenor saxophone sidemen included John Coltrane, Johnny Griffin and Charlie Rouse.

2. a. I was born on September 27, 1924 in New York City.
    b. I played and recorded with Cootie Williams in the early 1940s.
    c. My younger brother played piano with the Max Roach-Clifford Brown Quintet.
    d. One of my most unusual compositions is *"Glass Enclosure."*
    e. Dizzy Gillespie called me the "definitive pianist of the bebop era."

3. a. I was born around 1919 in Dallas, Texas and was raised in Oklahoma City.
    b. I was a regular participant in the legendary jam sessions at Minton's in Harlem.
    c. I played and recorded with the Benny Goodman Sextet between 1939 and 1941.
    d. I play trumpet, string bass and piano, but guitar is my main instrument.
    e. I was one of the first major soloists on amplified guitar.

4. a. I began my professional career as a pianist and arranger for bandleader Everett Hoagland.
    b. In 1941, my orchestra opened at the Rendezvous Ballroom in Balboa, California.
    c. My sidemen have included Art Pepper, Maynard Ferguson, Shelly Manne and Eddie Safranski; and vocalists June Christy, Chris Connor and Anita O'Day.
    d. I coined the term "progressive jazz."
    e. I was a pioneer in the jazz education movement.

5.   a.   I was born in 1940 in Fort Worth, Texas.
     b.   I attended Lincoln University in Jefferson City, Missouri, where I studied with David Baker.
     c.   I am a member of the World Saxophone Quartet.
     d.   My frequent recording mate is cellist Abdul Wadud.

6.   a.   I was born in 1920 in Concord, California.
     b.   I majored in music at the College of the Pacific.
     c.   At Mills College, I studied composition with Darius Milhaud.
     d.   My brother Howard is also a composer.
     e.   The saxophonist in my quartet was Paul Desmond.

7.   a.   I am a composer-drummer-pianist, who was born in 1923 in Cincinnati, Ohio.
     b.   I composed "*A Bird in Igor's Yard*" for Buddy De Franco.
     c.   I was on the faculty of the Lenox School of Jazz from 1958 to 1959.
     d.   I wrote "*Cubana Be Cubana Bop*" for Dizzy Gillespie's big band.
     e.   I am the author of *The Lydian Chromatic Concept of Tonal Organization for Improvisation.*

8.   a.   I was in two movies, *Higher and Higher* and *The Road to Zanzibar*.
     b.   In 1952, I formed my own record company, Debut.
     c.   I made my recording debut in 1947 with Lionel Hampton.
     d.   My autobiography is entitled *Beneath the Underdog*.
     e.   I am a bassist, composer and pianist.

9.   a.   I was born April 7, 1938 in Indianapolis, Indiana.
     b.   I attended Arsenal Technical High School.
     c.   I moved to New York City in 1958.
     d.   I played trumpet with Art Blakey, Quincy Jones and Sonny Rollins.
     e.   I was one of the trumpet players on one of Ornette Coleman's seminal free jazz recordings.

10. a.   I was born May 4, 1937 in Ferndale, Michigan.
     b.   I received my Bachelor of Music degree from the Eastman School of Music.
     c.   One of my first gigs was with the Chico Hamilton group that included Eric Dolphy.
     d.   In the 1970s, I began playing the piccolo bass in my quintet in addition to my regular instrument.

WHO AM I? (answers)

1. Thelonious Monk
2. Bud Powell
3. Charlie Christian
4. Stan Kenton
5. Julius Hemphill
6. Dave Brubeck
7. George Russell
8. Charles Mingus
9. Freddie Hubbard
10. Ron Carter

MATCH THE ORCHESTRA WITH ITS THEME SONG.

_____	1. Leo Reisman	a.	*I've Got a Right To Sing the Blues*
_____	2. Ozzie Nelson	b.	*Blue Nocturne*
_____	3. Chick Webb	c.	*Harlem Nocturne*
_____	4. Jack Teagarden	d.	*Jazznocracy*
_____	5. Dick Stabile	e.	*Loyal Sons of Rutgers*
_____	6. Randy Brooks	f.	*I May Be Wrong*
_____	7. Ray Anthony	g.	*Pastoral*
_____	8. Jimmy Lunceford	h.	*Redskin Rhumba*
_____	9. Charlie Barnet	i.	*Young Man with a Horn*
_____	10. Tony Pastor	j.	*Sleep*
_____	11. Bunny Berigan	k.	*When It's Sleepy Time Down South*
_____	12. Blue Barron	l.	*Ain't Misbehavin'*
_____	13. Ray Noble	m.	*I Can't Get Started with You*
_____	14. Fred Waring	n.	*Sometimes I'm Happy*
_____	15. Louis Armstrong	o.	*I'll See You in My Dreams*
_____	16. Fats Waller	p.	*Nightmare*
_____	17. Les Brown	r.	*Nighty-Night*
_____	18. Artie Shaw	s.	*Hot Lips*
_____	19. Henry Busse	t.	*What Is This Thing Called Love*
_____	20. Alvino Rey	u.	*Leap Frog*

MATCH THE ORCHESTRA WITH ITS THEME SONG
(answers)

1. t	11. m
2. e	12. n
3. f	13. o
4. a	14. j
5. b	15. k
6. c	16. l
7. i	17. u
8. p	18. d
9. h	19. s
10. g	20. r

44

WHAT INSTRUMENT IS PLAYED
BY EACH OF THE FOLLOWING ARTISTS?

1. Chano Pozo
2. Shelly Manne
3. Cannonball Adderley
4. Ray McKinley
5. Buddy Rich
6. David Baker
7. Leroy Vinnegar
8. Max Roach
9. Joe Venuti
10. Larry Ridley

11. Lionel Hampton
12. Rufus Reid
13. Andrew Hill
14. Marian McPartland
15. Frank Rosolino
16. Charles Lloyd
17. Clark Terry
18. Billy Strayhorn
19. Jimmy Smith
20. Andy Simpkins

WHAT INSTRUMENT IS PLAYED
BY EACH OF THE FOLLOWING ARTISTS? (answers)

1. Congas
2. Drums
3. Saxophone
4. Drums
5. Drums
6. Cello or trombone
7. Bass
8. Drums
9. Violin
10. Bass
11. Vibes, drums or piano
12. Bass
13. Piano
14. Piano
15. Trombone
16. Saxophone or flute
17. Trumpet
18. Piano
19. Organ
20. Bass

A.K.A.

By what name is each of the following artists better known?

1. Eleanor Gough McKay
2. Herbert Jay Solomon
3. Julius Gubenko
4. William DeBerardinis
5. Ian Ernest Gilmore Green
6. Locksley Wellington Hampton
7. George Joseph Hendleman
8. Jean-Francois Quievreux
9. Argonne Dense Thornton
10. Steven Lacritz
11. Peter Sims
12. Revoyda Frierson
13. Abdullah Ibn Buhaina
14. Melvin Sokoloff
15. Eugene McDuffy
16. Kenneth Norville
17. Anthony Dominick Benedetto
18. Herman Blount
19. Joseph Anthony Passalaqua
20. Norma Dolores Egstrom

A.K.A. (answers)

1. Billie Holiday
2. Herbie Mann
3. Terry Gibbs
4. Willie Dennis
5. Gil Evans
6. Slide Hampton
7. George Handy
8. Jef Gilson
9. Sadik Hakim
10. Steve Lacy
11. Pete LaRoca
12. Ketty Lester
13. Art Blakey
14. Mel Lewis
15. Brother Jack McDuff
16. Red Norvo
17. Tony Bennett
18. Sun Ra
19. Joe Pass
20. Peggy Lee

TRIVIA

1. Which of the following is **not** a bebop big band leader?
   a. Billy Eckstine
   b. Claude Thornhill
   c. Fletcher Henderson
   d. Dizzy Gillespie

2. Which characteristic is shared by boogie woogie and ragtime?
   a. Both are written music.
   b. Both are improvised music.
   c. Both are piano music.
   d. Both are big band music.

3. Which of the following is **not** an important swing band?
   a. the Tommy Dorsey band
   b. the Glenn Miller band
   c. the Andy Kirk band
   d. the Bunk Johnson band

4. Which of the following does **not** belong?
   a. Ornette Coleman
   b. Pharoah Sanders
   c. David Murray
   d. Horace Silver

5. Which of the following records was **not** a seminal record in the career of Miles Davis?
   a. *Bitches Brew*
   b. *Walkin'*
   c. *Kind of Blue*
   d. *Weather Bird*

6. The first important bebop trombonist was:
   a. Kid Ory
   b. Chu Berry
   c. J. J. Johnson
   d. Albert Ammons

7. The first jazz recordings were made in:
   a. 1921
   b. 1917
   c. 1931
   d. 1926

8. Which of the following is **not** a boogie woogie pianist?
   a. Cripple Clarence Lofton
   b. William Krells
   c. Meade Lux Lewis
   d. Freddie Slack

9. Which of the following is **not** a bebop piano player?
   a. Bud Powell
   b. Al Haig
   c. Thelonious Monk
   d. Lil Hardin Armstrong

10. Who was known as the "singing" bass player?
    a. Slam Stewart
    b. Jimmy Blanton
    c. Monk Montgomery
    d. Charles Mingus

TRIVIA (answers)

1. c
2. c
3. d
4. d. Horace Silver is the non- "new thing" player of the four. Also, the first three artists are saxophonists; Horace Silver plays piano.
5. d
6. c
7. b
8. b
9. d
10. a

MATCH THE BOOK
WITH THE ARTIST WHICH IS ITS SUBJECT

_____	1. *Beneath the Underdog*	a. John Coltrane
_____	2. *To Be, or Not . . . to Bop*	b. Dizzy Gillespie
_____	3. *Bird Lives*	c. Billie Holiday
_____	4. *Music Is My Mistress*	d. Anita O'Day
_____	5. *Raise Up Off Me*	e. Stan Kenton
_____	6. *Artistry in Rhythm*	f. Art Pepper
_____	7. *Lady Sings the Blues*	g. Charles Mingus
_____	8. *Somebody's Angel Child*	h. Duke Ellington
_____	9. *His Eye Is on the Sparrow*	i. Artie Shaw
_____	10. *High Times, Hard Times*	j. Bessie Smith
_____	11. *Straight Life*	k. Charlie Parker
_____	12. *The Stardust Road*	l. Ethel Waters
_____	13. *The Trouble with Cinderella*	m. Hoagy Carmichael
_____	14. *Of Minnie the Moocher and Me*	n. Cab Calloway
_____	15. *Chasin' the Trane*	o. Hampton Hawes

MATCH THE BOOK WITH THE ARTIST
WHICH IS ITS SUBJECT (answers)

1. g	9. l
2. b	10. d
3. k	11. f
4. h	12. m
5. o	13. i
6. e	14. n
7. c	15. a
8. j	

GIVE THE COMPOSER OF EACH
OF THE FOLLOWING GROUPS OF TUNES.

1. *Opus De Funk*
   Doodlin'
   Nica's Dream
   The Preacher

2. *Runnin' Wild*
   Old Fashioned Love
   If I Could Be With You
   Charleston

3. *How'm I Doin'?*
   Chant of the Weed
   Gee Baby Ain't I Good to You
   Cherry

4. *On a Misty Night*
   The Squirrel
   Lady Bird
   Our Delight

5. *Glass Enclosure*
   Wail
   Parisian Thorofare
   Dance of the Infidels

6. *I Saw Pinetop Spit Blood*
   Afro-American Sketches
   The Kennedy Dream Suite
   Blues and the Abstract Truth

7. *The Ballad of Hix Blewitt*
   Listen to the Silence
   Ye Hypocrite Ye Beelzebub
   Ezz-thetic

8. *Naptown Blues*
   Fried Pies
   West Coast Blues
   Jingles

9. *Sticks*
   Blues for Bohemia
   Marabi
   Them Dirty Blues

10. *The Chess Players*
    Lester Left Town
    Nefertiti
    Footprints

GIVE THE COMPOSER OF EACH
OF THE FOLLOWING GROUPS OF TUNES (answers)

1. Horace Silver
2. James P. Johnson
3. Don Redman
4. Tadd Dameron
5. Bud Powell
6. Oliver Nelson
7. George Russell
8. Wes Montgomery
9. Cannonball Adderley
10. Wayne Shorter

TRIVIA

1. Which of the following is **not** a vibraphone player?
   a. Lionel Hampton
   b. Red Norvo
   c. Milt Jackson
   d. Wardell Gray

2. Which of the following is **not** a Chicago jazzman?
   a. Bix Beiderbecke
   b. Frank Teschemacher
   c. Cab Calloway
   d. Gene Krupa

3. Which of the following does **not** belong?
   a. Maynard Ferguson
   b. Joe Masters
   c. Duke Ellington
   d. Mary Lou Williams

4. Which of the following does **not** belong?
   a. ragtime
   b. boogie woogie
   c. swing
   d. stride

5. Which of the following does **not** belong?
   a. sitar
   b. castanets
   c. bongos
   d. conga

6. Which of the following is **incorrect**?
    a. J. J. Johnson: trombone
    b. Ben Webster: saxophone
    c. Oscar Pettiford: bass
    d. Paul Desmond: piano

7. Which of the following is **not** an important date in the history of jazz?
    a. 1959
    b. 1917
    c. 1915
    d. 1920

8. Which of the following is **not** considered a seminal figure?
    a. Stan Getz
    b. Louis Armstrong
    c. Lester Young
    d. John Coltrane

9. Which of the following does **not** belong?
    a. spiritual
    b. field holler
    c. sonata
    d. work song

10. Which of the following does **not** belong?
    a. washtub bass
    b. kazoo
    c. jug
    d. oboe

TRIVIA (answers)

10. d. The oboe is a European instrument; the other three are ad hoc instruments.

9. c. The sonata is a European art music form; the other three are black American folk music forms.

8. a

7. c. 1917 was the year of the first jazz recording; 1920 the year of the first classic blues recordings; and 1959 the year that marked the beginnings of modal jazz and the arrival of Ornette Coleman in New York City.

6. d. Paul Desmond is a saxophonist.

5. a. All except the sitar are instruments associated with Latin music.

4. c. All are piano styles except swing.

3. a. All but Maynard Ferguson are associated with liturgical jazz.

2. c

1. d

A.K.A.

By what name is each of the following artists better known?

1. Louis Balassoni
2. Fritz Jones
3. Andreamenentania Paul Razafinkeriefo
4. John Cascales
5. Anthony Sciacca
6. Arthur Arshawsky
7. Edmund Gregory
8. Eunice Waymon
9. McKinley Morganfield
10. Saunders Teddell
11. Thomas Valentine
12. Sulaimon Saud
13. Vanig Hovsepian
14. Charles Jagelka
15. Khalil Yasin

A.K.A. (answers)

1. Louis Bellson
2. Ahmad Jamal
3. Andy Razaf
4. Johnny Richards
5. Tony Scott
6. Artie Shaw
7. Sahib Shihab
8. Nina Simone
9. Muddy Waters
10. Sonny Terry
11. Kid Thomas
12. McCoy Tyner
13. Turk Van Lake
14. Chuck Wayne
15. Larry Young

MATCH THE SINGER WITH THE SONG
WITH WHICH HE OR SHE IS ASSOCIATED.

_____ 1. Ella Fitzgerald   a. *Cry*

_____ 2. Bonnie Baker   b. *Let Me Off Uptown*

_____ 3. Billy Eckstine   c. *Nature Boy*

_____ 4. Doris Day   d. *A-Tisket, A-Tasket*

_____ 5. Nat "King" Cole   e. *Greenbacks*

_____ 6. Joe Williams   f. *Stormy Weather*

_____ 7. Louis Jordan   g. *Oh Johnny, Oh Johnny, Oh!*

_____ 8. Anita O'Day   h. *I Apologize*

_____ 9. Bessie Smith   i. *Sentimental Journey*

_____ 10. Johnnie Ray   j. *My Way*

_____ 11. Jimmy Witherspoon   k. *Every Day I Have the Blues*

_____ 12. Ray Charles   l. *Ain't Nobody Here But Us Chickens*

_____ 13. Teresa Brewer   m. *Gimme a Pigfoot*

_____ 14. Frank Sinatra   n. *Love Is a Five Letter Word*

_____ 15. Lena Horne   o. *Music! Music! Music!*

MATCH THE SINGER WITH THE SONG
WITH WHICH HE OR SHE IS ASSOCIATED (answers)

8. b	
15. f	7. l
14. j	6. k
13. o	5. c
12. e	4. i
11. n	3. h
10. a	2. g
9. m	1. d

IDENTIFY THE FOLLOWING ARTISTS
BY THEIR NICKNAMES.

1. Slide
2. Fatha
3. Count
4. Groove
5. Buster (clarinet)
6. Slam
7. P. C.
8. Klook
9. Sassy
10. Betty Bebop

11. Bags
12. Wes (guitar)
13. Hot Lips
14. Lucky (tenor saxophone)
15. Cat
16. Shorty
17. Red (vibes)
18. Red (bass)
19. Red (trumpet)
20. Wild Bill (trumpet)

IDENTIFY THE FOLLOWING ARTISTS
BY THEIR NICKNAMES (answers)

1. Locksley Wellington Hampton
2. Earl Hines
3. William Basie
4. Richard Arnold Holmes
5. William C. Bailey
6. Leroy Stewart
7. Paul Chambers
8. Kenny Clarke
9. Sarah Vaughan
10. Betty Carter
11. Milt Jackson
12. John Leslie Montgomery
13. Oran Page
14. Eli Thompson
15. William Alonzo Anderson
16. Milton M. Rogers, Shorty Sherock (Clarence Francis Cherock), or Harold Baker
17. Red Norvo (Kenneth Norville)
18. Keith Mitchell or George Callender
19. Red Rodney (Robert Chudnick) or Henry Allen
20. William Edward Davison

1. *If I'd Known You Were Comin' I'd Have Baked a Cake*
   Joe Venuti   Al Trace   Dominic Spera

2. *Naughty But Nice*
   Ray McKinley   Wayne King   Wayne Rogers

3. *Racing with the Moon*
   Larry Ridley   Vaughn Monroe   Ray Noble

4. *You're Nobody 'Til Somebody Loves You*
   Ted Dunbar   Russ Morgan   Abe Lyman

5. *The Very Thought of You*
   Don Thiele   Ray Noble   Ted Lewis

6. *I Was Meant for You*
   George Smith   Fats Waller   Noble Sissle

7. *Ain't Misbehavin'*
   Fats Waller   Wayne King   Count Basie

8. *Stardust*
   Albert Lerma   Hoagy Carmichael   George Russell

9. *I Cried for You*
   Al Jolson   Abe Lyman   Louis Prima

10. *When My Baby Smiles at Me*
    Ted Lewis   Mike Riley   Glenn Miller

11. *Josephine*
    Mike Lucroy   Wayne King   Duke Ellington

12. *It Had To Be You*
    Wayne King   Isham Jones   Glenn Miller

13. *It Isn't Fair*
    Richard Himber   April Baker   Carla Bley

14. *Flying Home*
    Dizzy Gillespie   Lionel Hampton   Count Basie

15. *I Wanna Be Loved*
    Harry James   Benny Goodman   Johnny Green

CHOOSE THE COMPOSER (answers)

8. Hoagy Carmichael
7. Fats Waller
6. Noble Sissle
5. Ray Noble
4. Russ Morgan
3. Vaughn Monroe
2. Ray McKinley
1. Al Trace

15. Johnny Green
14. Lionel Hampton
13. Richard Himber
12. Isham Jones
11. Wayne King
10. Ted Lewis
9. Abe Lyman

GIVE THE FAMILY NAME.

1. Wes, Buddy and Monk
2. Thad, Elvin and Hank
3. Tommy and Jimmy
4. Gene and Albert
5. Jimmy and Marian
6. Stanley and Tommy
7. Lester and Lee
8. Bud and Richie
9. Art, Evelyn and Art Jr.
10. Conte and Pete
11. Jackie and Rene
12. Budd and Keg
13. Earl and Bob
14. Urbie and Jack
15. Patti, Maxene and LaVerne
16. Ross and Don
17. Kenny and Bill
18. Art and Addison
19. Zoot and Ray
20. Chuck and Gap

GIVE THE FAMILY NAME (answers)

1. Montgomery		11. McLean	
2. Jones		12. Johnson	
3. Dorsey		13. Swope	
4. Ammons		14. Green	
5. McPartland		15. Andrews	
6. Turrentine		16. Barbour	
7. Young		17. Barron	
8. Powell		18. Farmer	
9. Blakey		19. Sims	
10. Candoli		20. Mangione	

MATCH THE ORCHESTRA WITH ITS THEME SONG.

_____	1. Cab Calloway	a. *That's What I Like About the South*
_____	2. Frankie Carle	b. *Flying Home*
_____	3. Benny Carter	c. *Dipsy Doodle*
_____	4. Gus Arnheim	d. *Minnie the Moocher*
_____	5. Buddy Moreno	e. *Let's Dance*
_____	6. Carmen Cavallaro	f. *Singing Wind*
_____	7. Freddy Martin	g. *Tonight We Love*
_____	8. Lionel Hampton	h. *Body and Soul*
_____	9. Tex Beneke	i. *Sunrise Serenade*
_____	10. Jan Garber	j. *Sweet and Lovely*
_____	11. Buddy Morrow	k. *Does Your Heart Beat for Me?*
_____	12. Larry Clinton	l. *Melancholy Lullaby*
_____	13. Benny Goodman	m. *It's That Time Again*
_____	14. Xavier Cugat	n. *Polonaise*
_____	15. Si Zentner	o. *Moonlight Serenade*
_____	16. Russ Morgan	p. *Night Train*
_____	17. Coleman Hawkins	r. *My Dear*
_____	18. Shep Fields	s. *My Shawl*
_____	19. Phil Harris	t. *Rippling Rhythm*
_____	20. Ralph Flanagan	u. *Up a Lazy River*

MATCH THE ORCHESTRA
WITH ITS THEME SONG (answers)

1. d	2. i	3. l	4. j
5. m	6. u	7. g	8. q
9. o	10. r	11. p	12. c
13. e	14. s	15. n	16. k
17. h	18. t	19. a	20. f

PUZZLE #4

The names of 17 important jazz artists are hidden in this
puzzle. Identify the artists from the clues given below; then go
to the puzzle diagram and locate their names. The names read
forward, backward, up, down, or diagonally. They are always
in a straight line and never skip letters. The names may
overlap and some letters may be used more than once, but not
all the letters in the diagram will be used.

K	A	Y	H	T	K	R	U	P	A
O	N	S	L	E	A	R	S	I	T
O	O	O	N	G	A	R	N	E	R
L	S	L	M	I	T	N	O	R	O
O	L	U	W	O	V	Y	T	C	N
G	L	N	R	T	S	L	N	E	T
U	E	I	Z	I	W	A	E	E	E
R	B	W	V	Z	F	A	K	E	R
T	B	A	H	E	F	T	I	R	R
A	D	Z	D	T	R	U	M	M	Y

Clues:

1. Trumpeter-bandleader who "mumbles"
2. Pianist-singer who often performed at Preservation Hall
   with her husband DeDe
3. Innovative composer-pianist born in Rocky Mount, North
   Carolina
4. Was the first to use mellophoniums in his band
5. Pianist-composer who never learned to read music
6. Drummer who is married to Pearl Bailey
7. Austrian pianist-composer who worked with Cannonball
   Adderley
8. Trombonist-singer who was a soloist with the Jimmie
   Lunceford band
9. Philadelphia-born pianist who worked with John Coltrane
10. Bobby Darin's personal drummer for four years
11. One of Stan Kenton's principal arrangers and a very

successful composer of music for television
12. A prolific film and television writer, his many credits include the ballad " *Li' l Darlin '* " and the music for the *Batman* television series
13. Bassist with the Eric Dolphy-Booker Little Quintet
14. Bassist who replaced Scott La Faro in the Bill Evans Trio
15. Michigan-born drummer who is the younger brother of Hank and Thad
16. Modern Jazz Quartet bassist
17. Chicago-born drummer who became famous with the Benny Goodman band and later led a successful big band of his own

PUZZLE #4 (answers)

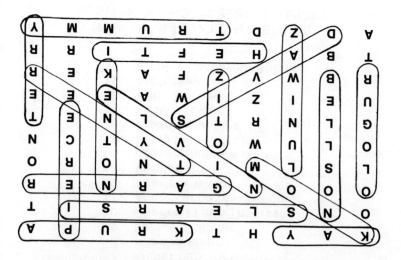

1.	Clark Terry	9.	McCoy Tyner
2.	Billie Pierce	10.	Ronald Zito
3.	Thelonious Monk	11.	Pete Rugolo
4.	Stan Kenton	12.	Neal Hefti
5.	Erroll Garner	13.	Richard Davis
6.	Louis Bellson	14.	Chuck Israels
7.	Josef Zawinul	15.	Elvin Jones
8.	Trummy Young	16.	Connie Kay
		17.	Gene Krupa

IDENTIFY THE FOLLOWING ARTISTS
BY THEIR NICKNAMES.

1. Swee'Pea
2. Chick (piano)
3. Cleanhead
4. Jabbo
5. Snooky
6. Trummy
7. Foots
8. Trigger
9. Lucky (bandleader)
10. Sir Charles

11. Dollar
12. Shadow
13. Bunky
14. Philly Joe
15. Miff
16. Hub
17. Mr. Five-By-Five
18. Lady Day
19. Buhaina
20. Luckey (piano)

IDENTIFY THE FOLLOWING ARTISTS
BY THEIR NICKNAMES (answers)

1. Billy Strayhorn
2. Armando Anthony Corea
3. Eddie Vinson
4. Gladys Smith
5. Eugene Edward Young
6. James Osborne Young
7. Walter Purl Thomas
8. Herman Alpert
9. Lucius Millinder
10. Charles Philip Thompson
11. Adolph Johannes Brand
12. Rossiere Wilson
13. Vernice Green
14. Joseph Rudolph Jones
15. Irving Milfred Mole
16. Freddie Hubbard
17. Jimmy Rushing
18. Billie Holiday
19. Art Blakey
20. Charles Luckeyeth Roberts

MATCH HUSBAND AND WIFE.

_____	1. Quincy Jones	a. Stokely Carmichael
_____	2. Phil Harris	b. Jayne Meadows
_____	3. Ray Brown	c. Nancy Wilson
_____	4. Jackie Cain	d. Jimmy McPartland
_____	5. Sarah Vaughan	e. Michael Mantler
_____	6. Cannonball Adderley	f. Cleo Laine
_____	7. Artie Shaw	g. Shirley Scott
_____	8. Stanley Turrentine	h. Bob Cooper
_____	9. June Christy	i. Roy Kral
_____	10. Red Norvo	j. Wayman Reed
_____	11. Alice McLeod	k. Peggy Lipton
_____	12. Kenny Dennis	l. Ella Fitzgerald
_____	13. Carla Bley	m. Mildred Bailey
_____	14. Marian Page	n. John Coltrane
_____	15. Miriam Makeba	o. Ava Gardner
_____	16. Steve Allen	p. Olga James
_____	17. John Dankworth	r. Alice Faye
_____	18. Hazel Scott	s. Herbie Kay
_____	19. Dorothy Lamour	t. Ozzie Nelson
_____	20. Harriet Hilliard	u. Adam Clayton Powell

MATCH HUSBAND AND WIFE (answers)

20. t	10. m
19. s	9. h
18. u	8. g
17. f	7. o
16. p	6. p
15. a	5. j
14. d	4. i
13. e	3. l
12. c	2. r
11. n	1. k

MATCH THE VOCALIST WITH THE BAND.

_____ 1. Eydie Gorme	a. Tony Pastor
_____ 2. Kay Starr	b. Jimmie Lunceford
_____ 3. Andy Russell	c. Spike Jones
_____ 4. Vaughn Monroe	d. Joe Venuti
_____ 5. Frank Sinatra	e. Tex Beneke
_____ 6. Helen Grayco	f. Gus Arnheim
_____ 7. Betty Hutton	g. Austin Wylie
_____ 8. Trummy Young	h. Harry James
_____ 9. Rosemary Clooney	i. Vincent Lopez
_____ 10. Marilyn Maxwell	j. Garwood Van
_____ 11. Dorothy Collins	k. Artie Shaw
_____ 12. Lena Horne	l. Dick Stabile
_____ 13. Georgia Gibbs	m. Noble Sissle
_____ 14. Jane Morgan	n. Ted Weems
_____ 15. Gale Storm	o. Raymond Scott
_____ 16. Art Carney	p. Count Basie
_____ 17. Roberta Lynn	r. Ted Lewis
_____ 18. Jo Ann Greer	s. Horace Heidt
_____ 19. Joe Williams	t. Sonny Burke
_____ 20. Ruth Etting	u. Henry Busse

MATCH THE VOCALIST WITH THE BAND (answers)

11. o	1. e
12. m	2. d
13. k	3. f
14. l	4. g
15. j	5. h
16. s	6. c
17. u	7. i
18. t	8. b
19. p	9. a
20. r	10. u

1. Name the "biggest band leader" (400 pounds!).
2. Who toured the nation with his "Musical Depreciation Revue"?
3. Which bandleader allowed numerology to dominate his life?
4. What is Raymond Scott's real name?
5. Who wrote "*Watermelon Man*"?
6. What singer is usually associated with a megaphone?
7. Whose orchestra was known as the "Hotsy-Totsy Orchestra" before it later adopted a more bubbly title?
8. With whose band did the Modernaires sing?
9. He wore a battered top hat and asked his audiences, "Is everybody happy?". Name him.
10. Name the all-girl orchestra led by the "Blonde Bombshell of Rhythm" and its leader.
11. Whose tag line was "The Twentieth-Century Gabriel"?
12. With whose orchestra did the King Sisters work?
13. What were the names of the Rhythm Boys?
14. Who wrote "*String of Pearls*"?
15. Who starred in the movie "*The Benny Goodman Story*"?
16. Who wrote "*Bumble Boogie*"?
17. Where and with whom did Duke Ellington celebrate his 70th birthday?
18. Who wrote "*Pennsylvania 6-5000*"?
19. Whose tag line was "The Ten Magic Fingers of Radio"?
20. Who was known as the "Rhumba King"?

MORE TRIVIA (answers)

1. Tiny Hill
2. Spike Jones
3. Vincent Lopez
4. Harry Warnow
5. Herbie Hancock
6. Rudy Vallee
7. Lawrence Welk
8. Glenn Miller
9. Ted Lewis
10. Ina Ray Hutton and Her Melodears
11. Erskine Hawkins
12. Horace Heidt or Alvino Rey
13. Bing Crosby, Al Rinker and Harris Barris
14. Jerry Gray
15. Steve Allen
16. Jack Fina
17. At the White House, with President Richard Nixon
18. Jerry Gray
19. Eddy Duchin
20. Xavier Cugat

64

IDENTIFY THE FOLLOWING ARTISTS BY THEIR NICKNAMES.

1. A. T. (drums)
2. Chick (drums)
3. The Empress of the Blues
4. Vice Prez (or Vice Pres)
5. The Divine One
6. Mr. B.
7. Big Mama
8. Big Joe
9. Little Esther
10. Muhal
11. Satchmo
12. Big Maybelle
13. Senator
14. Mwandishi
15. Fiddler
16. T-Bone
17. Toots
18. Sonny (drums)
19. Snub
20. Mahavishnu

IDENTIFY THE FOLLOWING ARTISTS BY THEIR NICKNAMES (answers)

1. Arthur Taylor
2. William Webb
3. Bessie Smith
4. Paul Quinichette
5. Sarah Vaughan
6. Billy Eckstine
7. Willie Mae Thornton
8. Joseph Turner
9. Esther Phillips
10. Richard Abrams
11. Louis Armstrong
12. Mabel Smith
13. Gene Wright
14. Herbie Hancock
15. Claude Williams
16. Aaron Walker
17. Jean Thielemans
18. William Greer, Gerald Brown or Owen Joseph Igoe
19. Leo Mosley
20. John McLaughlin

THE NAME'S THE SAME

1. U.S. president | Saxophonist-trumpeter | Bassist
2. *"In the Mood"* bandleader | *Death of a Salesman* author | Goldwater's running mate
3. U.S. president | Moody's scat singer | Sherman Hemsley's role
4. Actor | Bewitching actress | Guitarist
5. Polar explorer | Trumpeter | Guitarist
6. Confederate president | Trumpeter | Bassist
7. U.S. president | Trombonist | Tenor saxophonist
8. Civil rights leader | Tenor saxophonist | Former mayor of Atlanta
9. Lexicographer | Tenor saxophonist | Orator
10. Astronaut | Trumpeter | "All-American Boy"
11. Harlem politician | *Playhouse 90* actor | Bebop pianist
12. Scientologist | Trumpeter | Nursery rhyme mama
13. Playwright | Trumpeter | Clarinet-playing bandleader
14. U.S. president | Singer | Black educator
15. Singer-pianist | "The Thin Man" | Boxer
16. Comic book hero | Tenor saxophonist | Lucille Ball's TV boss
17. Bass player | Comic strip character | Former running back
18. Senate leader | Cool trumpet player | Jazz educator
19. Union leader | MJQ pianist | Author
20. Author of *The Lydian Concept of Tonal Organization for Improvisation* | Philosopher | Basketball player

THE NAME'S THE SAME (answers)

1. Jimmy Carter	Benny Carter	Ron Carter
2. Glenn Miller	Arthur Miller	William Miller
3. Thomas Jefferson	Eddie Jefferson	George Jefferson
4. Robert Montgomery	Elizabeth Montgomery	Wes Montgomery
5. Richard Byrd	Donald Byrd	Charlie Byrd
6. Jefferson Davis	Miles Davis	Richard Davis or Art Davis
7. Lyndon B. Johnson	J. J. Johnson	Budd Johnson
8. Whitney Young	David Young	Andrew Young
9. Noah Webster	Ben Webster	Daniel Webster
10. Neil Armstrong	Louis Armstrong	Jack Armstrong
11. Adam Clayton Powell	Dick Powell	Bud Powell
12. L. Ron Hubbard	Freddie Hubbard	Old Mother Hubbard
13. George Bernard Shaw	Woody Shaw	Artie Shaw
14. George Washington	Dinah Washington	Booker T. Washington
15. Ray Charles	Nick Charles	Ezzard Charles
16. Flash Gordon	Dexter Gordon	Gale Gordon
17. Ray Brown	Charlie Brown	Jimmy Brown
18. Howard Baker	Chet Baker	David Baker
19. John L. Lewis	John Lewis	Sinclair Lewis
20. George Russell	Bertrand Russell	Bill Russell

GIVE THE FAMILY NAME.

1. Bing and Bob
2. Benny and Harry
3. Buddy and Ella
4. Illinois and Russell
5. J. J. and Kevin
6. Arthur and Red
7. Jimmy, Albert and Percy
8. Donald and Albert
9. Wayne and Alan
10. Marty and Joe
11. Eloise, Hubert and Ronnie
12. Phil, Teddy and Marty
13. Dick and Ted
14. Chano and Chino
15. Joe and Foots
16. Stu and Claude
17. Ted and Milt
18. Wilbur and Sidney
19. Johnny and Baby
20. Les and Larry

GIVE THE FAMILY NAME (answers)

1. Crosby		11. Laws	
2. Goodman		12. Napoleon	
3. Johnson		13. Nash	
4. Jacquet		14. Pozo	
5. Johnson		15. Thomas	
6. Prysock		16. Williamson	
7. Heath		17. Buckner	
8. Ayler		18. De Paris	
9. Shorter		19. Dodds	
10. Marsala		20. Elgart	

WHO AM I?

1. a. I graduated from Virginia State College with a Bachelor of Music degree.
   b. During the 1940s, I worked with Dizzy Gillespie, Stuff Smith and Cozy Cole.
   c. I was one of the originators of the Jazzmobile in Harlem in 1965.
   d. I hosted the NPR show *"Jazz Alive."*

2. a. Although my parents were Australian, I was born in Toronto, Canada.
   b. I was an arranger for bandleader Skinnay Ennis.
   c. I was the principal arranger for the Claude Thornhill band between 1941 and 1948.
   d. I wrote the composition *"Boplicity."*
   e. I collaborated with Miles Davis on such albums as *Miles Ahead*, *Porgy and Bess* and *Sketches of Spain*.

3. a. I was born on January 17, 1937 in Port Arthur, Texas.
   b. I graduated from Texas Southern University in 1959 with a degree in pharmacy.
   c. I moved to Indianapolis, where I studied with David Baker and played guitar with Wes Montgomery.
   d. I am currently on the staff of Livingston College.

4. a. I was born in Brussels, Belgium.
   b. I record frequently with Quincy Jones.
   c. I wrote the tune *"Bluesette."*
   d. I not only play harmonica and guitar, but I also whistle professionally.
   e. My given name is Jean.

5. a. I was born on January 4, 1942 in Yorkshire, England.
   b. I played guitar with Tony Williams's *"Lifetime."*
   c. My former guru's name is Sri Chinmoy.
   d. I recorded *Bitches Brew* with Miles Davis.
   e. I was the leader of the Mahavishnu Orchestra.

6. a. My given name is John Leslie.
   b. I won a Grammy for my 1966 recording of *"Goin' Out of My Head."*
   c. I am a self-taught guitarist.
   d. My home is Indianapolis.
   e. Monk and Buddy are my brothers.

7. a. I am a bandleader and was born in 1913 in Milwaukee, Wisconsin.
    b. In 1936, I formed a co-operative band with key members of the defunct Isham Jones band.
    c. My original band became known as "The Band That Plays the Blues."
    d. In 1939, we had a hit with a composition by Joe Bishop called "*Woodchopper's Ball.*"
    e. Stravinsky's *Ebony Concerto* was written for me.

8. a. I am a bandleader-composer-saxophonist, who was born in 1913 near Faith, South Dakota.
    b. My bands were considered quite progressive and included such players as Dizzy Gillespie, Sonny Berman, Benny Harris, Earl Swope and Al Cohn.
    c. My arrangers included Ed Finckel, George Handy, Tadd Dameron and Johnny Richards.
    d. My band won the Esquire New Star Award in 1947.
    e. Some of my better-known recordings are "*Dalvatore Sally,*" "*March of the Boyds*" and "*Little Boyd Blue.*"

9. a. I am a singer, who appeared in the film *Pete Kelly's Blues*.
    b. I was once married to bassist Ray Brown.
    c. When Chick Webb died, I took over his band.
    d. I've shattered glass for Memorex.
    e. In 1938, I recorded "*A-Tisket, A-Tasket.*"

10. a. I am the female singer, who composed "*Downhearted Blues.*"
    b. In 1954-55, I was an understudy in the Broadway show *Mrs. Patterson*.
    c. Although I was born in 1897, I am still active as a performer in the 1980s.
    d. I was one of the first classic blues singers.
    e. I made my comeback at the Cookery in New York City.

WHO AM I? (answers)

1.	Billy Taylor	6.	Wes Montgomery
2.	Gil Evans	7.	Woody Herman
3.	Ted Dunbar	8.	Boyd Raeburn
4.	Toots Thielemans	9.	Ella Fitzgerald
5.	John McLaughlin	10.	Alberta Hunter

TV AND MOVIE MUSIC

Name the composer of the music for each of the following television shows or movies.

1. *Death of a Gunfighter*
2. *Barefoot in the Park* (movie)
3. *Cleopatra Jones*
4. *Death Wish*
5. *Blow-Up*
6. *In Cold Blood*
7. *A Man Called Adam*
8. *The French Connection*
9. *Mission: Impossible*
10. *In the Heat of the Night*
11. Closing theme from *All in the Family* ("*Remembering You*")
12. *Lady Sings the Blues*
13. *The Rifleman*
14. *A Warm December*
15. *The Six Million Dollar Man*
16. *The Karen Valentine Show*
17. *Anatomy of a Murder*
18. *Barefoot in the Park* (television series)
19. *The Black Frontier*
20. *The Pawnbroker*

TV AND MOVIE MUSIC (answers)

1.	Oliver Nelson	11.	Roger Kellaway
2.	Neal Hefti	12.	Michel Legrand
3.	J. J. Johnson	13.	Herschel Burke Gilbert
4.	Herbie Hancock	14.	Coleridge-Taylor Perkinson
5.	Herbie Hancock	15.	Oliver Nelson
6.	Quincy Jones	16.	Benny Golson
7.	Benny Carter	17.	Duke Ellington
8.	Don Ellis	18.	J. J. Johnson
9.	Lalo Schifrin	19.	David Baker
10.	Quincy Jones	20.	Quincy Jones

SOURCES UTILIZED

Balliett, Whitney. *New York Notes: A Journal of Jazz in the Seventies*. Reprint of the 1976 ed. published by Houghton Mifflin, Boston. New York: Da Capo Press, 1977.

Berendt, Joachim E. *The Jazz Book: From Ragtime to Fusion and Beyond*. Translated by H. and B. Bredigkeit with Dan Morgenstern. Westport, Connecticut: Lawrence Hill & Company, 1982.

Case, Brian, and Britt, Stan. *The Illustrated Encyclopedia of Jazz*. New York: Crown Publishers, Harmony Books, 1978.

Collier, James Lincoln. *The Making of Jazz: A Comprehensive History*. 1978. Reprint. New York: Dell Publishing Company, Delta Books, 1979.

Dance, Stanley. *The World of Swing*. Reprint of the 1974 ed. (v.1) published by C. Scribner's Sons, New York. New York: Da Capo Press, 1979.

Feather, Leonard. *The Encyclopedia of Jazz in the Sixties*. New York: Bonanza Books, 1966.

_____. *The New Edition of the Encyclopedia of Jazz*. New York: Bonanza Books, 1962.

Feather, Leonard, and Gitler, Ira. *The Encyclopedia of Jazz in the Seventies*. New York: Horizon Press, 1976.

Jewell, Derek. *The Popular Voice: A Musical Record of the 60s and 70s*. London: André Deutsch Limited, 1980.

Simon, George T. *The Big Bands*. Rev. ed. New York: Macmillan Publishing Co., Inc., Collier Books, 1974.

Taylor, Arthur. *Notes and Tones: Musician to Musician Interviews*. New York: G. P. Putnam's Sons, Perigee Books, 1982.

Taylor, Billy. *Jazz Piano: A History*. Dubuque, Iowa: Wm. C. Brown Company, 1983.

Walker, Leo. *The Big Band Almanac*. Pasadena, California: Ward Ritchie Press, n.d.

Wilmer, Valerie. *As Serious As Your Life: The Story of the New Jazz*. 1st U.S. ed. rev. Westport, Connecticut: Lawrence Hill & Company, 1980.

Jazz Studies and the Art Music

David Baker

★ ★ ★ ★ ★ ★ ★ ★ ★ ★ ★

NEW 1983 EDITION

JAZZ IMPROVISATION

For over a decade musicians everywhere have made this text their working bible. From fundamentals to advanced techniques, with pages of practice material in every chapter, plus provocative study questions and selected recordings, one of America's most gifted all-around musicians *and* teachers shares his knowledge with you.

Now published in a new, concise, up-dated edition ....

★ ★ ★ ★ ★ ★ ★ ★ ★ ★ ★

TECHNIQUES of IMPROVISATION
Vol. I, A Method for Developing Improvisational Technique ....
Vol. II, The II V7 Progressions ....
Vol. III, Turnbacks ....

ADVANCED IMPROVISATION
Vol. I, Improvisational Concepts ....
Vol. II, Rhythmic & Harmonic Concepts ....

ARRANGING & COMPOSING
(for the small ensemble) ....

★ ★ ★ ★ ★ ★ ★

A COMPLETE IMPROVISATION METHOD FOR STRINGED INSTRUMENTS
Vol. 1, Violin & Viola ....
Vol. 2, Cello & Bass Viol ....

JAZZ PEDAGOGY ....

JAZZ STYLES & ANALYSIS:
Trombone ....

Six Poemes Noir
pour Flute et Piano ....

ETHNIC VARIATIONS on a THEME of PAGANINI
based on CAPRICE XXIV Violin & Piano ....

SONATA I for Piano ....

SUITE Unaccompanied Violin ....

Singers of Songs – Weavers of Dreams
Solo Cello and Solo Percussion ....

SONATA Tuba and String Quartet ....

FRANGIPANI PRESS
P.O. Box 669
Bloomington, IN 47402